Discard

On Her Wings

~ THE STORY OF ~
TONI MORRISON

WRITTEN BY
JERDINE NOLEN

ILLUSTRATED BY
JAMES E. RANSOME

A PAULA WISEMAN BOOK

SIMON & SCHUSTER BOOKS FOR YOUNG READERS

NEW YORK LONDON TORONTO SYDNEY NEW DELHI

SIMON & SCHUSTER BOOKS FOR YOUNG READERS
An imprint of Simon & Schuster Children's Publishing Division
1230 Avenue of the Americas, New York, New York 10020
Text © 2022 by Jerdine Nolen
Illustration © 2022 by James E. Ransome
Book design by Laurent Linn © 2022 by Simon & Schuster, Inc.
For information about special discounts for bulk purchases, please contact Simon & Schuster Special Sales
at 1-866-506-1949 or business@simonandschuster.com.
The Simon & Schuster Speakers Bureau can bring authors to your live event. For more information or to book an event,
contact the Simon & Schuster Speakers Bureau at 1-866-248-3049 or visit our website at www.simonspeakers.com.
The text for this book was set in ArrusBT Std.
The illustrations for this book were rendered in watercolor and collage.
Manufactured in China
0522 SCP
First Edition
2 4 6 8 10 9 7 5 3 1
Library of Congress Cataloging-in-Publication Data
Names: Nolen, Jerdine, author. | Ransome, James, illustrator.
Title: On her wings : the story of Toni Morrison / Jerdine Nolen ; illustrated by James E. Ransome.
Description: First edition. | New York : Simon & Schuster Books for Young Readers, [2022] | "A Paula Wiseman Book." |
Audience: Ages 4-8. | Audience: Grades 2-3. | Summary: "Born Chloe Ardelia Wofford, she grew up listening to stories and loved reading.
As a teenager she worked at the Lorain town library and later attended Howard University. As an editor at a New York publisher,
she found time early in the morning and late at night after her children were asleep to write. When she looked about over her life and
all what she had seen and learned, she knew she wanted to write about her people, Black people.
Today and always her work and legacy will live on"— Provided by publisher.
Identifiers: LCCN 2021008156 (print) | LCCN 2021008157 (ebook) | ISBN 9781534478527 (hardcover) | ISBN 9781534478534 (ebook)
Subjects: LCSH: Morrison, Toni—Juvenile literature. | Novelists, American—20th century—Biography—Juvenile literature. |
African American novelists—Biography—Juvenile literature.
Classification: LCC PS3563.O8749 Z787 2022 (print) | LCC PS3563.O8749 (ebook) | DDC 813/.54 [B]—dc23
LC record available at https://lccn.loc.gov/2021008156
LC ebook record available at https://lccn.loc.gov/2021008157

For all artists who look past the distraction to keep doing the work
—J. N.

To my dear friend Jerry Pinkney
—J. E. R.

You know . . .

I believe that girl could fly
on the wings of words
whenever she had a mind to.

When Toni Morrison was born, her parents called her Chloe Ardelia Wofford. Chloe had three siblings. Lois was first. Chloe came eighteen months later. The girls were always very close. They had two younger brothers, George and Raymond.

Long before Chloe became a reader or writer, she was a listener.

Chloe loved to listen to her mother, father, and grandparents tell stories. She also loved hearing the music they made—the singing and violin- and clarinet-playing going on in the house. There were stories of the Bible, the myths and legends. Her parents told ghost stories and tales of the supernatural. For Chloe the tales were frightening, thrilling, full of music and adventure—stories that were at times painful, beautiful, and wise—sometimes all at once. She learned those stories and retold them to others.

chloe was little then, just a-listening. . . .

As she was growing up, those words and stories and music lit up with magic and meaning inside Chloe. Rhythms and lyrics and verses and texts surrounded Chloe and stirred up her storytelling imagination.

The stories opened
windows into her heart
and allowed doorways to open
onto the heart of the world.

Her hometown of Lorain, Ohio, was much too poor and too small to be segregated, so Chloe went to Hawthorne Elementary School with children from many different countries. Some were just learning English. She was the only student in her first-grade class who could read, and she read well. Chloe loved reading. She was often asked to read with those who needed help.

She didn't let it bother her too much that her teachers couldn't pronounce her name easily.

There were words and music in the air.

Chloe continued to read more and more, feeding a hunger that would never end.

Chloe's mother was a member of the African Methodist Episcopal Church, but many in Chloe's extended family were Catholic. Chloe was close to a cousin who was Catholic. At twelve years old Chloe decided to convert to Catholicism. She chose Saint Anthony of Padua, patron saint of lost things, as her baptismal name. So now she was Chloe Anthony Wofford.

In the 1940s there were not many jobs for teenagers. But kids could clean other people's homes or work in their kitchens for three or four hours a day. Housekeeping was Chloe's first job. She earned two dollars a week. One dollar was for her mother. She kept the other.

The second job she held was at the Lorain Public Library. She was so happy to be surrounded by books. She was supposed to put the returned books back on the shelves. Every shift started with a tall stack of books—fiction, history, drama, poetry—everything. With so many different books, she couldn't help it. She'd open a book, and before long she would be lost in the story. She had to get a different job.

It didn't matter. Chloe's library work was a doorway to a freedom that was life-changing and kept her coming back for more books to read.

Stories lifted her.

She was just a-listening, waiting, watching.

Chloe did well in high school. She was involved in many activities. She was a library aide, class treasurer, and member of the National Honor Society, and she was involved in yearbook and drama. Her father, George Wofford, worked as a welder in the shipping yard. He taught his children to work hard and take pride in their accomplishments. Because reading, education, and learning were important to the Wofford family, it was certain Chloe would attend college.

At Howard University her friends had a difficult time with her name too. So she told them to just call her "Toni." She went on to Cornell University for graduate work and then taught at Texas Southern University. She later returned to Howard to teach English. There she met and married Harold Morrison, an architect.

Chloe and Harold Morrison

HOWARD UNIVERSITY

CORNELL UNIVERSITY

One day
she would take those old tales
that told the history of the world

and use them
to tell her own stories.

After the birth of Chloe and Harold's firstborn, Harold Ford,
Chloe joined an on-campus writers group. Her marriage ended
just before the birth of her second son, Slade. She made a new
start. She left Howard University and began working as an
editor in New York. Her sister, Lois, came along for support.
Her future was being shaped. It was her turning point.

And . . . she started to write.

During the day, she worked as an editor to publish other writers' stories. At night, after she put her children to bed, she started to write her own stories. She saw a beginning. But for a writer the question always is: What do I want to write about?

When she looked back over her life after all she had seen and learned, she knew she only wanted to write stories about her people, Black people, specifically African American mothers and their children in their communities and their families. She placed mothers and children front and center in the heart of her novels. Many people asked her, "Why?" She simply answered, "Why not!"

When she was thirty-nine years old, her first novel, *The Bluest Eye*, was published. But she wasn't happy when her editor put the name "Toni Morrison" on the cover. She felt herself to be Chloe Wofford. "Toni" was only a nickname.

I'm telling you, that girl was *magic*.

As the years passed, Toni Morrison published many, many books and won many, many important awards. It was when she won the Nobel Prize in Literature that she said, "It was Chloe, by the way, who went to Stockholm last year to get the Nobel Prize." She was the first African American woman to receive the award.

Toni Morrison wrote about the history and pain of Black life in the United States. The stories she told were so hard to talk about and so very hard to tell, but she did. She wrote about slavery. She wrote about the hard times for Black people after slavery ended, and their struggles to make a place for themselves in the world. She had learned from her parents and grandparents and great-grandparents the language of fearlessness and dignity and, above all, to love and value yourself.

It was as if she could look beyond things as they were and see a greater vision. Inside the world created in her books, she sought to empower and heal, especially around the topic of skin color. She showed that it was just fine that people come in many different colors.

of oppression

and pull against each thread until the blanket just unraveled.

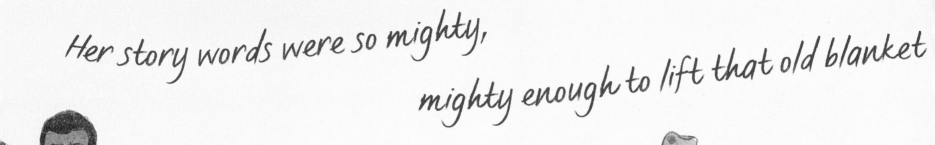

Her story words were so mighty,

mighty enough to lift that old blanket

That girl held the mirror of light
and understanding in her hands,
shining it, reflecting it
onto the people of the world.

It was as if she could look beyond things as they were, and tell the untold stories that needed to be told. And then she showed us how to let go, take to the air and fly, soaring above the hurt to gain a new understanding of our lives—of all people.

That girl was filled with magic.

Her stories radiated poetry, liberty, wonderment, and light.

With all the light that dwelled inside her, she lit a way to understanding and acceptance. She paid attention, listened well, and told us what she saw—what she heard.

Then she went on to shine that light
so others could see,
so others could tell.

Now you, go on. You tell your stories!

❀ ❀ ❀

Years ago, when I picked up my first Toni Morrison novel, *The Bluest Eye,* I remember I was very excited. I cuddled in my cozy overstuffed chair one rainy afternoon, expecting to read until dinner. I didn't. I couldn't get past the first four pages. On the one hand, the text was familiar. It made me chuckle a bit for days gone by. I'd read the Dick and Jane (and Sally) primers in elementary school. On the other hand, using it in this way as a structural device made me feel . . . uneasy. Those stories of Dick and Jane were a monument to my childhood, yet there was a whole section of text in the novel where there were no spaces between the words and there was no punctuation. It created not only concern in me but an urgency. Something was wrong. Something was very wrong. And I wasn't sure I wanted to know what it was. I put the book down and walked away.

As humans, we are so hungry for stories. We want to know about other people's lives even if they are just characters in a book. And we make comparisons between ourselves and the characters we are reading about. Sometimes these comparisons cause us to live differently.

The four pages brought back memories of my elementary school days. I was reminded of a particular reproduction of a famous painting that hung in the hallway on the way to the office. It was the Dalí painting of the melting watches stretched out over a landscape. I always slowed my steps as I neared it. The painting didn't make sense. Watches don't melt. It made me feel nervous. And the stories of Dick and Jane and Sally always had spaces between those familiar words and there was *always* punctuation.

Reading the four pages restimulated a childhood fear of mine. But I was an adult now. I told myself: This is literature. Reading is a change agent. Maybe I didn't understand what I was reading. I thought about the fix-up strategies I have shared with my students when comprehension breaks down: Read it again. Read it aloud. Ask questions of the text.

A lengthy conversation followed.

Without any effort on my part, the book magically opened up to chapter two. Softly my eyes fell upon the words on that page, and I slowly began reading. Immediately I was immersed in the rhythm and poetry of the language, the phrasing of the words, and the gentle matter-of-fact tone that was so soothing, I felt I was being cradled through the hard parts and the pain that dripped from the pages. Later in the book, I found myself returning to certain sections to reread just because what was happening to Pecola was so unbelievable or the language was just too exquisite not to read again and again—it hurt.

Since then I have approached reading many of Toni Morrison's novels much in the same way. There has been a time or two when I hurled a book across the room and left it there. But each time I went to retrieve it, eventually letting the magic and music of the words wash over me and open up my mind and heart to a new or another perspective.

When I began to write this book on Toni Morrison, I decided to start with her name, as the fact that her name changed and the way she felt about the change completely intrigued me. I thought it was very symbolic. As I started to draft the text another voice seemed to be floating around just above my head—*You know, I believe that girl could fly. She could . . . on the wings of words . . . she could soar.* The voice sounded like I remembered my grandmother sounding. She had the long sight of some other side of things. She would speak clear out of the blue, which caught me off guard but made me think deeper. I felt I had to honor what I heard. Those are the words that float on each page.

Spiritualism and the supernatural permeate Toni Morrison's novels. Symbolically, Bible stories show up in her novels. She often used the literary form of sermon—the words formed out of fear and trembling, but always intertwined with grace and mercy at the heart of the story for purposes of healing, perhaps with the hope and expectation that we would live differently.

In her film, *Toni Morrison: The Pieces I Am*, Morrison is quick to tell us her realization of the power of words and language came from the elders of the family household, including a grandfather who was a "reading revolutionary." During his young life, it was illegal for him to read and write. And, because of his illegal activity, he would brag that he had taught himself to read the Bible enough times that he had memorized parts of it. Her mother encouraged storytelling and writing, but stopped Lois and Chloe just in time from copying certain words someone had written on the sidewalk that shouldn't be known. Reading, writing, and listening are powerful.

They, together, are change agents.

And that is what Toni Morrison did for us. With the power of her words and the way she used language, she changed everything—for the better.

LEARN MORE ABOUT TONI MORRISON

Official Website of the Toni Morrison Society: **tonimorrisonsociety.org**

BOOKS FOR YOUNG READERS
CHILDREN'S BOOKS WRITTEN WITH SLADE MORRISON

1999	*The Big Box*
2002	*The Book of Mean People*
2003	*Who's Got Game? The Ant or the Grasshopper?*
2003	*Who's Got Game? The Lion or the Mouse?*
2003	*Who's Got Game? Poppy or the Snake?*
2004	*Remember: The Journey to School Integration* (written without Slade Morrison)
2009	*Peeny Butter Fudge*
2010	*Little Cloud and Lady Wind*
2011	*The Tortoise or the Hare*
2014	*Please, Louise*

NOVELS

1970	*The Bluest Eye*
1973	*Sula*
1977	*Song of Solomon*
1981	*Tar Baby*
1987	*Beloved*
1992	*Jazz*
1997	*Paradise*
2003	*Love*
2008	*A Mercy*
2012	*Home*
2015	*God Help the Child*

IMPORTANT QUOTES

ON IDENTITY

"The very serious function of racism . . . is distraction. It keeps you from doing your work. . . ."
—"A Humanist View," a 1975 speech Morrison gave at Portland State University

ON WRITING

"A writer's life and work are not a gift to mankind; they are its necessity."
—*The Source of Self-Regard*, 2019

"Words have power."—*The Pieces I Am*, 2019

"Language alone protects us from the scariness of things with no names. Language alone is meditation." —Toni Morrison's Nobel lecture, 1993

QUOTES FROM NOVELS

"Beauty was not simply something to behold; it was something one could *do*." —*The Bluest Eye*

"It is sheer good fortune to miss somebody long before they leave you." —*Sula*

"If you surrendered to the air, you could ride it." —*Song of Solomon*

"A dead hydrangea is as intricate and lovely as one in bloom. Bleak sky is as seductive as sunshine, miniature orange trees without blossom or fruit are not defective; they are that."
—*Tar Baby*

"Freeing yourself was one thing; claiming ownership of that freed self was another." —*Beloved*

"What's the world for you if you can't make it up the way you want it?" —*Jazz*

"There is honey in this land sweeter than any I know of, and I have cut cane in places where the dirt itself tasted like sugar, so that's saying a heap." —*Paradise*

"Love is or it ain't. Thin love ain't love at all." —*Love*

FILM AND VIDEO

Greenfield-Sanders, Timothy, dir. *Toni Morrison: The Pieces I Am*. 2019.

Harvard Divinity School. "Have Mercy: The Religious Dimensions of the Writings of Toni Morrison." December 6, 2012. https://hds.harvard.edu/news/2012/12/11/have-mercy-religious -dimensions-writings-toni-morrison.

OF INTEREST

Als, Hilton. "Ghosts in the House: How Toni Morrison Fostered a Generation of Black Writers." *New Yorker*, October 19, 2003. https://www.newyorker.com/magazine/2003/10/27/ghosts-in -the-house.

Dreifus, Claudia. "CHLOE WOFFORD Talks About TONI MORRISON." *New York Times*, September 11, 1994. https://www.nytimes.com/1994/09/11/magazine/chloe-wofford-talks -about-toni-morrison.html.

Morrison, Toni. "Goodness: Altruism and the Literary Imagination." 2012 lecture at Harvard Divinity School. *New York Times*, August 7, 2019. https://www.nytimes.com/2019/08/07/books /toni-morrison-goodness-altruism-literary-imagination.html.

Morrison, Toni. Nobel lecture, December 7, 1993. https://www.nobelprize.org/prizes /literature/1993/morrison/lecture.

Morrison, Toni. "Tell City Leaders to Invest in Libraries." New York Public Library blog, May 1, 2018. https://www.nypl.org/blog/2018/05/01/toni-morrison-tell-city-leaders-invest -libraries.

Nittle, Nadra. "The Ghosts of Toni Morrison: A Catholic Writer Confronts the Legacy of Slavery." *America Magazine*, November 3, 2017. https://www.americamagazine.org/arts -culture/2017/11/03/ghosts-toni-morrison-catholic-writer-confronts-legacy-slavery.

Peet, Lisa. "Celebrated Author Toni Morrison, Who Centered the Black Experience in Literature, Dies at 88." *Library Journal*, August 6, 2019. https://www.libraryjournal.com /?detailStory=celebrated-author-toni-morrison-who-centered-the-black-experience-in -literature-dies-at-88.

SELECT ACHIEVEMENTS AND INFORMATION

1977	Won the National Book Critics Circle Award for *Song of Solomon*
1985	Joined NYPL Board of Trustees; named Life Trustee in 2006
1988	Received the Pulitzer Prize and the American Book Award for *Beloved*
1993	Awarded the Nobel Prize in Literature—the first African American woman to be honored
1996	Honored with the National Endowment for the Humanities' Jefferson Lecture
1996	Received the National Book Foundation's Medal for Distinguished Contribution to American Letters
2011	Awarded the Library of Congress Creative Achievement Award for Fiction
2012	Presented with the Presidential Medal of Freedom by President Barack Obama
2016	Dedicated a bench at NYPL's Schomburg Center for Research in Black Culture in Harlem to honor its role in archiving, preserving, and sharing the Black experience
2016	Received PEN/Saul Bellow Award for Achievement in American Fiction
2016	Recognized with the Gold Medal for Fiction from the American Academy of Arts and Letters

Morrison held teaching positions at Bard College, SUNY Albany and SUNY Purchase, and Howard, Yale, Rutgers, and Princeton universities. At Princeton, she was the Robert F. Goheen Professor in the Humanities. Her papers have been collected and selectively digitized at Princeton's Harvey S. Firestone Memorial Library.

In honor of Morrison's contribution to Princeton, the university dedicated Morrison Hall, formerly West College, in 2017.